WITHDRAWN

DATE DUE

Fidel Castro

Fidel Castro

CUBAN REVOLUTIONARY

BRENDAN JANUARY

FRANKLIN WATTS
A Division of Scholastic Inc.
New York Toronto London Auckland Sydney
Mexico City New Delhi Hong Kong
Danbury, Connecticut

Photographs © 2003: AP/Wide World Photos: cover left, 30, 91 (Jose Goitia), 88 (Paul Hanna), 68 (Cristobal Herrera), 95 (Liborio Noval/Granma, Pool), 65 top (U.S. Department of Defense), 19, 53, 57, 65 bottom, 79, 81; Corbis Images: 47, 98 (AFP), 10, 13, 25, 41, 45, 59, 70 (Bettman), 87 (Richard Bickel), 22 (Tim Page), 86 (Peter Turnley), 33 (Robert Van der Hilst), 43 (Baldwin H. Ward); Getty Images: 2 (Cristobal Herrera-Pool), 15 (Jorge Rey); Hulton | Archive/Getty Images: 26, 28, 36, 61, 76, 101; Magnum Photos: 71 (Ian Berry), 49 (Burt Glinn), 63 (Bob Henriques); Nik Wheeler: 12; South American Pictures/Rolando Pujol: 74.

Library of Congress Cataloging-in-Publication Data

January, Brendan, 1972–
   Fidel Castro: Cuban revolutionary / by Brendan January.
     p. cm. — (Great life stories)
   Includes bibliographical references and index.
   ISBN 0-531-11676-X

1. Castro, Fidel, 1927—Juvenile literature. 2. Cuba—History—1959—Juvenile literature. 3. Cuba—Relations—United States—Juvenile literature. 4. United States—Relations—Cuba. 5. Revolutionaries—Biography—Juvenile literature. 6. Heads of state—Cuba—Biography—Juvenile literature. [1. Castro, Fidel, 1927– 2. Heads of state. 3. Revolutionaries. 4. Cuba—History—1959– 5. Cuba—Relations—United States. 6. United States—Relations—Cuba.] I. Title. II. Series.

F1766.22.C3 J36 2001
972.9106'4—dc21
                                                                           00-043546

03085 8268

Contents

Fidel Castro was born near Birán in eastern Cuba. Cuba is the largest island in the Caribbean Sea.

ONE

Birth of a Revolutionary

On August 13, 1926, a baby was born to a serving maid and a landowner in eastern Cuba, a slender island nation less than 100 miles (160.9 kilometers) from Florida. It was a boy. His parents named him Fidel. His last name was Castro Ruz.

By the time the boy had grown up and ruled Cuba, he would be known around the world as "Fidel Castro." Castro would later tell a priest that he was born early in the morning, at 2 A.M. Being born in darkness, said Castro, suited him for guerrilla fighting.

CASTRO'S FAMILY

Fidel Castro's father, Angel, was originally from Spain. He grew up in the rocky, barren land of Galicia. At age twenty, Angel joined the Spanish army and in the late 1890s was sent to fight the U.S. citizens in Cuba.

After the war, Angel settled in Cuba. Despite having no money or prospects, Angel prospered. First he sold glasses of lemonade to thirsty workers. Then he organized workers to cut wood for a local sugar mill owned by an American. Later, he became the boss of fifty sugarcane cutters. Angel was ruthless, unsentimental, and determined.

When Angel had grown rich, he built a giant house called Las Manacas near the village of Birán. He bought surrounding pieces of land to enlarge his estate. Angel also used less legal methods to expand his property. At night, Angel and his men would extend the farm by moving his fences into unsettled areas. His holdings swelled to 10,000 acres (4,050 hectares) and hundreds of workers labored in his fields.

From Angel's rough clothes and simple shoes, a visitor would have difficulty distinguishing him from the peasants who worked for him. But he always carried a silver-handled whip and never went into the fields without his Colt .45 revolver. Angel refused to deposit his money in banks, preferring instead to keep it secure in a lockbox in his home.

Angel was already married when Lina Ruz, Fidel's mother, became a servant at Las Manacas. Angel and Lina started a love affair, and Lina began having Angel's children. When Angel's first wife discovered the affair, she left him.

Fidel grew up surrounded by his brothers, sisters, and the chickens, ducks, and turkeys that roamed freely in the yard. The house was constructed on stilts with a staircase leading to the front door that could be removed to act as a barrier against attacking robbers. At night, milk cows were tethered beneath the house.

Lina Ruz fixed a giant meal each day in the kitchen and announced its completion by firing a shotgun. Servants, family members, and field hands crowded together around a large pot on the stove and ate standing up. For the rest of his life, Fidel would be most comfortable eating food with his hands.

Angel ruled his farm strictly and harshly, traits that Fidel learned to imitate. But neither his father nor his mother imposed much discipline on the young Fidel, who spent his time mingling freely with the field hands who worked for his father and their children.

Castro would speak warmly about his mother, but said he was never close to his father. He recalled that he knew almost nothing about the man, his ambitions, or his past. In a 1985 interview, Castro said, "I do not know much [about my father's] first years. I didn't feel the curiosity that I might feel today." A biographer of Castro observed that Castro had plenty of time to learn about his father if he had wanted to.

When Was Castro Born?

Throughout his life, Fidel Castro concealed the details of his youth. Historians aren't even certain what year he was born. Castro said he was born in 1926. His sisters say it was 1927. When Castro wrote a letter to Franklin Delano Roosevelt in 1940, he said he was twelve years old—indicating that he was born in 1928.

Fidel did, however, enjoy being the son of a landowner and usually got what he wanted. He played with the field hands' children. In baseball games, Fidel brought the equipment and demanded that he be the pitcher. If he lost or played poorly, he threw a temper tantrum and took the equipment home.

Fidel developed a love of firearms that lasted his entire life. He grew up in a society where violence was an accepted method for resolving disputes, and death caused by a gun or knife was not uncommon. Fidel

Workers cut sugarcane in a Cuban field in 1920s. Harvesting sugarcane is exhausting work, and the field hands usually received low wages for their efforts.

would spend hours hunting in the forests and mountains around his home and was delighted by target practice.

Later, Fidel developed a nostalgic attachment to his childhood and the countryside. "If it depended on me," he would later say, "I would always be in the country. I prefer it a thousand times to the city."

In this wild environment, Fidel learned to color his language with curses and never seemed to hold back when he wanted to speak his mind. Once, when he tripped and cut his tongue on a nail, his mother told him it was punishment for his foul language.

Fidel also attributed his concern for the poor to his early years, when he noticed that most of his playmates lived in squalor. During the season when the laborers cut sugarcane or worked in the fields, they brought home enough money to feed their families. However, during the time where there was no work, called the "dead time," they had to survive on what they had.

Fidel's upbringing was also filled with stories about Cuba, its fascinating history, and its glorious heroes. He learned that the island had deep connections to the United States.

AN ISLAND NATION

Cuba was one of the landmasses first spotted by Christopher Columbus on his famous voyage in 1492. He claimed the land for Spain, and the Spanish settlers arrived in the early 1500s to rule the island. Through disease and harsh work policies, the Spanish quickly reduced Cuba's original fifty thousand inhabitants to five thousand. In the 1700s, the Spanish imported tens of thousands of African slaves to grow the crop that would become the lifeblood of the Cuban economy, sugarcane. By 1860, the island's population had reached more than 1.3 million, almost half of it made up of slaves imported from Africa and their descendants. Cuba produced more than one-third of the world's sugar.

Visitors were stunned by Cuba's beauty. In the lush, tropical temperatures, plants of all kind flourished, keeping the landscape a deep green color for most of the year. The spines of several mountain ridges rose out

Cuba is known for its rich, green landscapes. The country receives between 40 to 70 inches of rain each year, which helps keep the countryside beautiful.

of the island. Farmers in the mountains grew bananas, corn, tobacco, and coffee. The valleys and plains along the sea were covered with fields of sugarcane. When the cane grew more than 6 feet (1.8 meters) high, armies of workers wielding large, heavy knives called machetes entered the fields for the harvest.

The Spanish rulers were repressive, corrupt, and inefficient. Because of the imposition of high taxes and a lack of representation in the Spanish government, the Cubans revolted and declared their independence in 1868. Ten years of warfare followed and ended in a stalemate. The Spanish gave Cuba some political representation in the government, but would not give the island the right to rule itself. Slavery was abolished in 1886.

During this period, Cuba, which was so close that it could almost be seen from Florida, attracted the interest of the United States. In 1823, the United States created the Monroe Doctrine, a decree that told Europe to

Born in 1853, José Martí was killed in a battle with Spanish troops.

stay out of the Western Hemisphere. Any attempt to set up colonies there would be viewed as an act of aggression against the United States. While warning Europe to stay away, U.S. citizens invested millions of dollars in agriculture in Cuba, and U.S. politicians vainly tried to buy Cuba from the Spanish several times.

When José Martí led a Cuban revolt for independence in 1895, people in the United States watched closely. The bloody war dragged on for three years, with neither side gaining an advantage. In 1898, the United States sent a battleship, the U.S.S. *Maine,* to the Cuban capital city, Havana. The battleship was meant to protect U.S. citizens living in Cuba. On February 15, a mysterious explosion rocked the ship and sent it to the bottom of the harbor. More than 250 American sailors died.

U.S. newspapers printed headlines that blamed the Spanish for the disaster. Urged by the press, the United States declared war on Spain. In four months, the U.S. army and navy won several spectacular victories that forced the Spanish to ask for peace. Both the Cubans and the Americans celebrated the victory, but when the Americans marched into Santiago, they raised the U.S. flag, not the Cuban one. This act was humiliating for Cuban nationalists. Worse, on December 10, 1898, the Treaty of Paris gave control of the island nation to the U.S. military.

It took the United States three years to turn over power to the Cubans. Still, U.S. officials didn't trust the Cubans to run their own affairs. Before a Cuban leader was elected, Congress created the Platt Amendment. The amendment gave the U.S. government the right to intervene in Cuba when it judged appropriate to secure order and progress. It also retained a naval base at Guantanamo Bay on the south-eastern coast of Cuba. By the time the amendment was nullified in

1934, the United States had sent troops to Cuba three times—in 1906, 1912, and 1917—to quell unrest that threatened U.S. economic interests. Cubans, both rich and poor, deeply resented the arrogance of the "Colossus of the North."

U.S. dominance in Cuba was economic as well as political. U.S. citizens owned most of the island's sugar factories. Havana, the nation's cultural and political center, became a popular tourist spot, where U.S. citizens flocked to gamble, drink, and enjoy the tropical weather.

While the United States bans its citizens from traveling to Cuba, people from around the world visit Havana to enjoy its tropical climate and culture.

The U.S. government generally supported Cuban leaders who kept the country stable. Few, if any, Americans cared that most Cuban leaders were as corrupt as the Spanish rulers who were overthrown in 1898. The price of sugar rose through the early part of the century and many Cubans prospered. However, the majority of Cubans, especially those living in the countryside, lived in poverty with no access to schools or hospitals.

SCHOOL DAYS

As the son of a wealthy landowner, however, Fidel had opportunities other Cubans did not. The most important one was a good education. When Fidel turned five, Angel abruptly sent him to Santiago de Cuba, a city on the southern coast, to be entered in a Catholic school run by priests. Fidel missed his family and playmates. In his first night in the city, he wet his bed.

Despite the troubled beginning, Fidel wasn't intimidated by his surroundings for long. He soon demonstrated traits that would appear throughout his life—stubbornness, an explosive temper, and ruthlessness when dealing with others.

In playground games, he demanded to play the best positions. On lines, he jostled and pushed to be first. Teachers forced him to scrawl "I'll behave in line" and "I will not talk in class" thousands of times on the chalkboard. When he failed to memorize a poem, a teacher reprimanded him. Infuriated, Fidel turned all the desks in the classroom upside down and tried to convince his fellow students to strike.

Joined by his brothers, Raúl and Rámon, Fidel earned a reputation as one of the worst bullies in the school. When the priests complained to

Fidel's father, Angel ordered the three boys to return to Las Manacas. Suddenly, Fidel realized the importance of his education. He threw a tantrum and threatened to burn down the house if he didn't get his way and return to school.

His parents gave in, and Fidel was sent back to Santiago, this time to a Jesuit school. Still, the young boy could hardly stand the hours of classes, which he later described as similar to being in a cage. He longed to go outside to play or listen to his radio. The other boys, the sons of wealthy aristocrats, treated the brash and ill-mannered Fidel with contempt. Fidel only won acceptance on the playground, where his energy and competitive nature were recognized and celebrated.

Later in his life, Castro described himself as an accomplished scholar. "I was one of the best in the class, I passed the entrance exam and entered high school."

His classmates, however, recall it differently. Fidel struggled through school, missing assignments, avoiding reading, and cramming before tests, which he did easily because of his excellent memory. His favorite subject was history. He engrossed himself in tales of Cuban heroes and revolutionaries, especially José Martí, who was killed by Spanish soldiers after leading a force ashore in 1895 to liberate Cuba.

When Fidel received poor grades, he stole a blank report card from the teachers, wrote in his own grades, and forged the signatures of his guardians on the original. Castro's parents were delighted that their son was doing so well in school.

Fidel Castro's young life is filled with stories of tantrums and angry words. "One day I stood up to the lady of the house and told her off about the way they had treated me," he recalled about a place in which he lived while attending school. "I told them all to go to the devil."

Fidel also took himself very seriously. When Franklin Delano Roosevelt was elected president for a third term in November of 1940, Fidel Castro wrote him a letter of congratulations.

"I am a boy, but I think very much," Fidel wrote in broken English. "If you like, give me ten dollars bill green american in the letter, because I have not seen a ten dollars bill american and I would like to have one of them."

Fidel was disappointed when he received a reply that the U.S. government could not spare him the money.

A Passion for History and the Military

In Santiago, Fidel's guardians locked him in his room after school so he would do his homework, but he would not give in. He resolved not to study, and instead he fashioned strips and balls of paper on a small board and pretended they were armies. "There were losses, casualties," he later recalled. "I played this game of wars for hours at a time."

Fidel's interest in history and the feats of great heroes extended into religion. He was forced to attend mass every morning for several years. Of all the Bible stories he read, he most enjoyed the ones that featured battles, such as the one in which the walls of Jericho collapsed before Joshua's army.

When he was sixteen years old, Fidel moved to Havana with his older sister, Angela, to enter another academy. Again, Fidel was surrounded by wealthy students who ridiculed his rough manners and foolish clothes and called him "peasant" behind his back.

When Fidel showed up to play basketball, the coach rejected him. Angered, Fidel practiced dribbling, shooting, and passing the ball for an entire year. He set up lights so he could practice at night. By the end of high school, Fidel was captain of the team. But in his fierce desire to win, he sometimes forgot which side he was playing on. During one game, he scored in the wrong basket.

Fidel loved debating and won a school prize. But he could not tolerate disruptions during his debates. Once, he was interrupted by a judge during the middle of a speech. Enraged, Fidel slammed his fist down on a table and cracked the marble top.

The priests in his school called him, *El loco Fidel,* or "crazy Fidel." Fidel's

Fidel makes a speech on state intervention in education. This photograph appeared in Fidel's 1945 school year book.

actions often justified the nickname. One day, he argued with another student about whether he could ride a bicycle into an iron door to force it open. Finally, Fidel accepted a dare and tried it at full speed. The door did not yield an inch, and Fidel spent three days in the infirmary.

In 1945, Fidel graduated from high school. He was eighteen years old, 6 feet (2 m) tall and weighed more than 190 pounds (86 kilograms). It was time for his next move, which was to go to Havana for university studies and to discover the calling that would define his life.

From Student
to Radical

Castro moved into an apartment in September of 1945 with two of his sisters and lived off a generous monthly stipend provided by his father. As he began his studies at the University of Havana, Castro had no special interest in studying law. As an eighteen-year-old young man without a strong interest in one profession, law seemed to be a good enough option. Some friends told him that he was suited for law because he enjoyed talking so much.

"He talked politics all the time, *all* the time," recounted Max Lesnick, a close friend, "with a very, very grandiose and, at the same time, idealistic scheme of how to run the country, how to improve things. He did it with a great deal of passion, emotion, vehemence—convincing people."

University life was filled with politics. Students fiercely debated the roles of government and society. Students formed groups dedicated to

At the University of Havana, Castro was more interested in politics than his studies.

revolution and social reform. The groups argued with one another, but they also used violence and assassination to get their way.

Castro, who grew up surrounded by firearms and the macho environment of the countryside, felt right at home. Obsessed with becoming a student leader, he joined the Insurrectional Revolutionary Union (UIR), one of the strongest student groups on campus, and began carrying a pistol.

For the most part, Castro was unsuccessful in his efforts to become a leader. Students were repelled by his poor hygiene, quick temper, and irrepressible ego. A conversation with Castro was usually one-sided, with Castro delivering his message for hours and not tolerating interruption.

Castro did more than just talk. Declaring that he wanted "to have a line written about me in Cuban history," Castro joined a military expedition to overthrow a hated dictator in the nearby Dominican Republic in 1947. After the freighter carrying 1,200 armed volunteers set sail, it was captured by the Cuban government. The men were loaded onto a naval vessel to be returned to Havana. As Castro later described it, he jumped overboard, swam through shark-infested waters, and walked 20 miles (32 km) to his boyhood home, Las Manacas.

In April of 1948, Castro headed a delegation of students sent to Colombia for an economic conference. Only days after Castro's arrival, a popular Colombian leader was assassinated, plunging the capital city into riots. Castro couldn't resist joining the angry mobs as they roamed the streets, smashing and overturning cars and setting them ablaze. Later, Colombian politicians would accuse Castro and another Cuban of inciting the riots, but Castro denied the charges.

Castro was gaining a reputation as a wild, unpredictable character with a fierce passion and a willingness to use violence to get his way. In the bloody turf wars between student groups, Castro was implicated in two murders. Again, Castro denied any involvement.

The following autumn, Castro returned to the University of Havana to begin another semester. When the local bus company tried to raise fares, Castro organized protests that involved the burning of buses. The company backed down.

In October, Castro began settling into a more stable life. He married Mirta Díaz Balart, a philosophy student at the university. The couple honeymooned in the United States and settled in the Bronx. He flirted with the idea of attending Columbia University, but political events in Cuba soon drew him back to Havana.

Many members of the Cuban government were corrupt. The elected rulers used their power to enrich themselves and their circle of close allies and friends. Despite having one of the highest tax rates in Latin America, the government couldn't pay its debts. Instead, millions of dollars were looted from the treasury, and officials lived in spacious mansions and drove American luxury automobiles.

Disgust with the abuses of power led to the creation of the Ortodoxos Party, a political party that promised fairness in government. After settling in a Havana apartment with his new wife, Castro became one of Ortodoxos's first members.

Castro soon had a small family. In September of 1949, his wife gave birth to a son named Félix Fidel Castro Díaz, or "Fidelito." Castro also continued to study law. His acute memory allowed him to avoid attending classes and studying until he needed to cram for final exams. He graduated in 1950.

Castro had little interest in his profession. For two years, he tried few cases and his law practice languished. He also paid little attention to his family, and Mirta and Fidelito were often literally left in the dark when Castro forgot to pay the electric bills. Instead, Castro focused on politics. Hoping to represent Havana in the Cuban congress, he campaigned aggressively, making dozens of speeches against government corruption.

BATISTA COMES TO POWER

As the June 1952 elections approached, the political parties scrambled to make alliances to ensure themselves a role in the government. The Ortodoxos, however, decried the corruption and refused to make deals. As it turned out, the parties never had a chance anyway. Early on the morning of March 10, Cuban soldiers took over radio and television stations in Havana. A former Cuban president and general, Fulgencio Batista

This photograph shows Fidel with his son Fidelito.

y Zalvidar, declared himself the new leader of Cuba. The president, Carlos Prío Socarrás, called on the Cuban people to resist and then fled to Mexico. With the support of the army, Batista bloodlessly and easily seized power.

The new dictator quickly curtailed freedom of press and speech. Members of opposing political parties were harassed or arrested. The

With the support of the military, Batista took over the government of Cuba in 1952. He is shown here with his wife at a meeting of a women's political party.

guarantees of freedom promised by the Cuban democracy, corrupt as it was, melted away.

Still, the country seemed relieved. Considering the previous state of the government, some Cubans hoped that Batista would be an improvement. Castro, who nurtured dreams of political success, was devastated. He returned to the university and urged the students to join him in armed revolt. He wrote an angry manifesto that ended with the line from the national anthem "to live in chains is to live in shame; to die for the Fatherland is to live." The students, however, were not persuaded by Castro's passion. Finally, Castro took some pistols, ammunition, and a machine gun, and left home with a small group of dedicated followers. On March 24, he filed a brief in court declaring Batista's coup to be illegal. He was ignored.

Castro, however, would not give up. In May of 1952, he called for an armed rebellion to a group of students. "Revolution opens the way to true merit to those who have sincere courage and ideas," he said, "to those who risk their lives and take the battle standard in their hands."

He returned to Las Manacas and asked his father for money to buy weapons. Angel did not attempt to conceal his disgust. "It's really stupid to think that you and that group of starving ragamuffins could bring down Batista, with all his tanks, cannons, and airplanes," he said.

Castro had hoped his father would give him $4,000. He left with $140. Not everyone rejected Castro's requests for money. A doctor sold his private plane and donated the $10,000 to Castro's cause. It was, however, a solitary success, and most wealthy Cubans turned Castro away.

In the meantime, the Batista regime became more repressive. Although Batista had promised to allow free elections, he kept postponing them. Individuals and any political organization that did not support Batista were quickly and brutally crushed.

Castro labored on, traveling around Cuba to recruit men and women to join his cause. His faith in himself was boundless. "Fidel had this way of captivating people," said Gerardo Pérez Puelles, one of Castro's followers. "Maybe it was the warmth of his speech. He could get together with ten guys and he would have ten more recruits. He was very, very good at this."

Castro had a way of talking that drew people to him and got them interested in his causes.

Castro's followers tended to come from the middle and lower classes, those who had little hope or felt unfulfilled. They couldn't resist his enthusiasm and his belief that his own success was inevitable, despite the tiny size of their movement.

"When we were barely a small group that didn't even number ten, Fidel was already the leader," remembered Melba Hernandez, one of Castro's earliest volunteers. "And we didn't feel as though we were ten, we felt like a movement of tremendous force."

As the Batista government became more repressive, Castro had more success recruiting followers. On the hundredth anniversary of Cuban revolutionary José Martí's birth, hundreds of Castro's followers, called *Fidelistas*, marched through downtown Havana carrying blazing torches.

ATTACK ON MONCADO BARRACKS

Castro wasn't satisfied with marching. In the spring of 1953, he began to plan an attack on an army barracks at Moncado, which was located in the southeast corner of the country. The barracks, home to about 1,400 soldiers, held vast quantities of arms, ammunition, and equipment. The fact that Castro commanded only about two hundred rebels did not discourage him. He would exploit confusion and surprise to seize the barracks and its radio station. After the rebels broadcast news of the attack, Castro hoped Cuba's people would rise in revolt against the hated Batista. Even if the rebels were defeated, their attack would be a bold and inspiring stroke. Castro planned the assault for July 26, when the area would be celebrating fiesta and most of the soldiers and residents would be slumbering after a night of parties.

As the date drew nearer, Castro gathered shotguns, Browning sub-machine guns, carbine rifles, and other military supplies, while revealing little to his men. On July 25, more than two hundred rebels congregated in a farmhouse outside Santiago.

That evening, Castro revealed the plan in a fiery speech. At the end of his talk, he said, "You joined the movement voluntarily, the same is true of this attack." His followers were stunned, scared, excited, and, to Castro's fury, reluctant. Ten dropped out. The rest pulled on olive green army uniforms and tied black sashes around their arms to distinguish themselves from Batista's men. Castro was too excited to sleep.

At 5 A.M., in the gray darkness just before dawn, the attack force set off for the Moncado barracks in a roaring column of twenty-six automobiles. Castro sat in one of the cars, carrying his rifle. His brother, Raúl, followed. According to Castro's plan, he and eighty-nine men would capture the barracks while Raúl seized the nearby Palace of Justice.

Raúl Castro played an important role in Fidel Castro's revolutionary movement and has served as a top official in the Cuban government. This photograph shows Fidel and Raúl during a meeting of the Cuban National Assembly in 2001.

The first car pulled up in front of the barracks. Renato Guitart, one of Castro's followers, yelled at the guards, "Attention! Attention! Let the general in!" The three soldiers, sleepy and confused, snapped to attention. The rebels swarmed over them, knocking one to the ground. But the other two managed to alert the garrison. Events soon exposed serious faults in Castro's plan, among them the lack of a good map. Castro's men rushed to the armory but discovered a barbershop instead.

Hundreds of soldiers, now awake and alert, opened fire on the attackers. Castro, who had been further back in the convoy, arrived and realized the attack had failed. Another car full of his heavily armed rebels was lost in Santiago's maze of streets and never showed up. Raúl successfully occupied the Palace of Justice, but Castro had already ordered the rebels to withdraw. He never fired a shot.

The rebel group disintegrated. At least eight dead and twelve wounded men were left at the barracks. Others escaped to Havana. Castro and about twenty followers hurried by foot into nearby hills, where they hoped to find refuge. Those who were captured were tortured and shot by Batista's furious, vengeful soldiers. Castro evaded capture for a week. On August 1, an army patrol discovered Castro asleep in a peasant's hut.

The patrol's commander, Lieutenant Pedro Sarriá, refused to bring Castro to the Moncada barracks, where Castro certainly would have been executed. Instead, he sent him to the local prison. There, sitting alone in a cell, Castro was protected from death by public opinion. The public had become enraged by Batista's executions of the revolutionaries.

Castro's plans for the attack may have been disastrous, but his prediction that defeat would still result in victory was accurate. The assault

Moncada: A Successful Failure

For the rest of his life, Castro would give speeches on the anniversary of the attack on the Moncada barracks. In his remarks, Castro would refer to the skirmish as a necessary defeat. In 1963, on the tenth anniversary of the attacks, he said, "The great significance of this date lies in the fact that on that day, our people began, on a small scale—if people say so—to embark on a road leading to revolution. . . . We did not manage to take the Moncada barracks at the time, but we remained firm in our confidence. We firmly believed that that was the road and undertook the task of pushing the struggle forward on the basis of more mature experience. Finally the correctness of the road was borne out by history, facts, and life."

made Castro a folk hero among the Cuban people.

In September of 1953, Castro and the other rebel leaders were put on trial. Castro defended himself, ending the trial with a speech that listed his proposed reforms to the government. He promised to reduce rents and give struggling farmers the chance to own their own farms. He would attack the malnutrition, unemployment, and high illiteracy rates that crippled Cuba's poor.

He concluded with a ringing declaration. "As for me, I know that imprisonment will be . . . filled with threats, ruin and cowardly deeds of rage, but I do not fear it, as I do not fear the fury of the wretched tyrant who snuffed out the lives of seventy brothers of mine. Condemn me, it does not matter. History will absolve me."

Castro, twenty-seven years old, was sentenced to fifteen years in prison. Castro was sent to the Isle of Pines, an island off Cuba's south coast. Twenty-nine others, including Raúl and two female followers, received sentences ranging from several months to thirteen years.

TIME IN PRISON

Prison life could have been worse for Castro. As a political prisoner, he was allowed privileges. He could send and receive letters and was allowed to exercise and cook his own meals on a small stove. Castro filled the hours by organizing an education program for himself and his fellow prisoners. The prison authorities also allowed him to receive packages of food.

In one letter, he described his routine with enthusiasm. "What a terrific school this prison is!" he wrote. "Every morning at 9:30 and at 10:30, I lecture about philosophy or world history. Other comrades teach Cuban history, grammar, arithmetic, geography, and English. At

This is a photograph of the jail cell where Castro served his prison sentence.

night I handle political economy and, two times a week, public speaking, if you can call it that."

Castro requested books from his friends—novels by Victor Hugo, Honoré de Balzac, Fyodor Dostoyevsky, Leo Tolstoy, philosophy by Saint Thomas Aquinas, Karl Marx, Vladimir Lenin, and the complete works of William Shakespeare.

"Whenever I read a book by some famous author, the history of a people, the teachings of some thinker, or the writings of a social reformer," Castro wrote to Natalia Revuelta, "I am seized by the desire to comprehend all the works of all authors. . . . When I was outside I fretted because I had no time, but even here, where time seems more than abundant, I still worry."

Castro's relationship with his wife, Mirta, had cooled off long before his prison term. In his letters to her, he only asked for favors and inquired about the health of their son, Fidelito. In 1954, Castro discovered that Mirta had taken a job in the Batista government. Her decision formally ended the marriage by divorce in December of 1954.

By then, Batista had held his long-promised election in November. According to his results, he had won by a huge majority. Confident in the afterglow of the victory, Batista announced that he'd grant freedom for all political prisoners.

On May 15, 1955, Castro and nineteen other veterans of the attack on the Moncada barracks were released from the Isle of Pines. Neither his imprisonment nor the disaster at Santiago had humbled Castro's ambitions. He made plans to continue his movement, which he now named the 26th of July Movement, in honor of the ill-fated attack on the Moncada barracks.

Castro spent his first months of freedom attacking the Batista regime in newspapers and on radio and television programs. To Castro's disgust, the old political parties were in shambles, torn apart by petty strife and arguing, and couldn't mount any resistance against Batista. Batista's police watched Castro closely, and Castro began to fear he would be assassinated. Realizing he could not mount a revolution under such oppression, Castro left Cuba on July 7, 1955, for Mexico. He vowed to return to his native land in triumph.

More people, including Ernesto "Che" Guevara (above), became interested in Castro's movement. Guevara came from a middle-class family in Argentina, and had earned a M.D. degree from the University of Buenos Aires before joining Castro.

THREE

"My Comrades and I Are Here to Liberate Cuba"

Several dozen of Castro's comrades—the core of the 26th of July Movement—followed him to Mexico. But life there was often worse than life in Cuba. The Mexican police were suspicious of the Cubans, especially because many were living in the country illegally.

Impatient and insecure, Castro desperately tried to keep in touch with Cuban politics. "I'm being driven crazy, wanting to know how things are going there," he wrote to a friend in Cuba. "I feel more isolated than when they had me in solitary confinement."

Castro set out to gather the money he needed to buy the guns, ammunition, and equipment he would need to invade Cuba and bring down the Batista regime.

"We do not mind if we have to beg for the Fatherland," said Castro. "We do so with honor." Still, even begging did little. When Castro asked an American pilot to fly weapons to Cuba, the man demanded $7,500. Castro had only $20.

Castro embarked on a fund-raising tour. He spent seven weeks in the United States visiting Cuban exiles. In New York, Philadelphia, and Miami, he convinced Cuban groups to support his vision of the revolution and raised several thousand dollars.

Castro also attracted followers. One of them, Ernesto "Che" Guevara, was a young doctor from Argentina who would play a critical role in the Cuban Revolution. He met Castro in July of 1955 and, like so many others, was immediately impressed by Castro's passion and conviction.

Guevara, along with Castro's men, trained for the invasion. They took long hikes in Mexico City's giant Chapultepec Zoological Park. In April of 1956, Castro moved his men to a ranch outside Mexico City. There, they learned how to clean and handle rifles and make bombs. They also learned the tactics of guerrilla warfare.

Castro was careless in his preparations. In June of 1956, police discovered a store of his equipment, including personnel files on the Cuban rebels and their invasion plans. Castro and several of his men were thrown in jail. They were released, but on the condition that they leave the country within two weeks.

Taking greater care to conceal themselves, the rebels continued training. In September, Castro received $50,000 from the former Cuban president, Prío Socarrás. Castro used $20,000 to buy a weathered wooden yacht named *Granma*. Castro did not have much more time. The Mexican police captured more of his men, rifles, and 15,000 rounds of ammunition.

Fearing more police raids, Castro moved up his date for the invasion to November 25. It had been seventeen months since he'd left Cuba's shores.

CASTRO RETURNS TO CUBA

On the night of November 24, 1956, Castro waited impatiently alongside the *Granma* in the Mexican port city of Tuxpan. Finally, after midnight, Castro ordered eighty-two men to board the 65-foot (19.8-m) vessel. As it drizzled around them, the men crowded boxes of food, weapons, and ammunition onto the deck. At 1:30 A.M., Castro ordered the *Granma* to leave port. The engines pushed the overloaded boat out of Tuxpan and into the Gulf of Mexico. Consulting his compass, Castro ordered the ship to head due east. He expected to land in Cuba within five days.

The *Granma* pitched and rolled in the choppy seas. Many of the men grew sick while others hummed a revolutionary hymn to calm their nerves. Dressed in green fatigues with a pistol slung under his arm, Castro cheerfully encouraged his followers.

The trip took longer than Castro had calculated. By December 1, the men huddled aboard the ship, tired, thirsty, and hungry. Castro had planned to coordinate his landing with revolts in Cuba scheduled for November 30. Castro listened helplessly to radio reports saying that revolts had flared briefly, but had been crushed by Batista's forces.

On December 2, the *Granma* ran aground in a tangle of treacherous swamps in the Oriente Province on the southeastern coast of Cuba. The men prepared to land by loading supplies into a smaller boat. The vessel, its hull pockmarked with holes, sank almost immediately. Castro and his men had no choice but to wade ashore. After leaving their machine guns, radio, and medical equipment on the boat, the men hefted their rifles over their heads and struggled for hours through the muck.

Soon after reaching solid ground, the party discovered a lone peasant. Castro placed his hand on the man's shoulder.

"My comrades and I are here to liberate Cuba," he announced in a loud voice. "You have nothing to fear from us, who have come expressly to help the peasants, giving them lands to work, markets for their products, schools for their children, and a healthy way of life for the entire family."

Batista had been alerted to Castro's landing by the failed rebellion on November 30, and his forces began to search for the invaders. Castro spent three days leading his men toward the protection of the mountains. Batista's planes hovered overhead with speakers that broadcast a message guaranteeing the rebels fair treatment if they surrendered.

Many were tempted. Most of the supplies had been left on the beach, and Castro's men were exhausted. Daily rations were half a sausage and two crackers. To avoid the army troops who were searching for them, the men traveled at night and hid during the day. Thirsty, they cut raw sugarcane and sucked on the stems. Batista's pursuing soldiers easily followed the trail of chewed sugarcane stalks.

On December 5, a group of Batista's soldiers surrounded Castro and his men as they rested in a small grove of trees. The soldiers opened fire. Surprised, Castro's men scattered in a panic. Guevara was hit in the neck. Others tried to hide among rows of nearby sugarcane. Four rebels were killed and almost all their remaining equipment was left behind.

Cuban army troops arrive to search the mountains for Castro and his followers.

Castro's army, now shattered into tiny groups, continued toward the mountains. On December 13, Batista announced that the rebels had been destroyed and withdrew his forces from the region.

Castro and two companions survived. On December 17, the trio reached an isolated farmhouse owned by a supporter of the movement. Over the next few days, more survivors trickled in, each time greeted enthusiastically by their companions. By all accounts, though, the landing had been a complete disaster. Of the eighty-two men who landed, only seventeen remained, including Castro's brother, Raúl, and Che.

After the men rested and enjoyed a hearty meal, their confidence began to return. Castro spoke eagerly of his plans and, once again, victory seemed inevitable.

"We'll win the war!" exclaimed Castro. "We're just beginning to fight!"

Later, however, Castro would admit, "A struggle could not have begun under worse circumstances."

INTO THE MOUNTAINS

The rebels had no knowledge of the mountains they planned to use as their base. No passable roads penetrated the thick vegetation and treacherous slopes. Supplies had to be carried up and down narrow dirt trails on the backs of animals.

The terrain proved to be a blessing. The rebels found it difficult to maneuver, but the army units sent to pursue them found it nearly impossible. In the peaks and valleys of the mountains, sheltered in its morning mists, Castro's tiny revolutionary group began to grow.

In the meantime, protests against Batista's rule became more common, and the government reaction to these events more cruel. Hundreds of students were rounded up and held without trial after bombs exploded in Havana. When protestors were captured, many were tortured, executed, and their bodies left hanging from trees and lampposts.

Castro began to attack isolated army units and garrisons. Early in the morning of January 17, the rebels surrounded a small army post at La Plata on Cuba's southern coast. Castro told the fifteen soldiers to give up, but they refused and began firing their guns. Two of Castro's men crawled to the buildings and set them aflame, forcing the soldiers to surrender. Castro's men suffered no casualties and captured valuable stores of provisions, ammunition, and medical supplies.

As Castro continued his attacks, he and his men became more confident and skilled in guerrilla warfare. Still, press censorship was strict, and few people in Cuba knew that Castro was even still alive. To publicize his growing campaign, Castro arranged an interview with Herbert

Cuba's dense vegetation and rough terrain made it easier for Castro and his troops to hide from Batista's soldiers.

Matthews, a reporter from *The New York Times*. On February 17, Castro and Matthews talked for several hours, and Matthews later published the interview in three long articles.

Castro carefully arranged the setting to impress the journalist. Although he commanded only twenty men, Castro tried to look like the leader of a powerful, extensive, and efficient revolutionary force. Castro ordered his soldiers to march back and forth through the camp while he spoke to Matthews, thereby multiplying the size of his army. He ordered another follower to interrupt his conversation with important sounding information. "Commandante, the liaison from Column Number Two has arrived," the follower solemnly told Castro in front of Matthews.

Matthews was completely taken in. "Fidel Castro, the rebel leader of Cuba's youth, is alive and fighting hard and successfully," he wrote. "[Castro is] the most dangerous enemy General Batista has yet faced."

Copies of Matthews's articles were smuggled into Cuba, and word spread among the population that Castro not only lived, but his movement flourished. Matthews described the bearded Castro as a dashing leader in his green army fatigues, smoking an endless chain of cigars. He wrote about Castro's favorite rifle, one made in Belgium with a telescopic sight. Each of Castro's men wore the patch of the 26th of July Movement on his shoulder.

"From the look of things," wrote Matthews, "General Batista cannot possibly hope to suppress the Castro revolt."

Following Matthews, journalists from all over the world ventured into the Sierra Maestra region of Cuba to interview the rebel leader. As Castro's fame grew, so did his army, and life in the mountains was becoming pleasant. Castro passed much of his time comfortably, lying in his hammock with a stack of books nearby.

On April 19, Batista's generals announced that Castro's army had been routed out of the mountains. Castro soon proved it otherwise. On May 28, he led his men on an attack at El Uvero, where a fifty-soldier garrison was stationed. After heavy fighting, the soldiers surrendered. Casualties were high on both sides—fourteen dead and nineteen wounded in the army and six of the rebels dead and nine wounded. Guevara jubilantly stole a truck crammed full of supplies and drove it back into the mountains.

The victory had stunning consequences. Enraged, Batista declared war on the rebels and sent reinforcements to the region. Matthews returned to Cuba, interviewed Castro, and wrote another glowing article that proclaimed Castro to be "stronger than ever."

A journalist from Spain, Enrique Meneses, Jr., described how Castro ruled in the rebel camp. "While we sat around a campfire," he observed,

Castro explains his political objectives to freelance journalist Enrique Meneses, Jr.

"Fidel Castro would pace up and down like a bear, his hands behind his back, expounding his plans for the future. Everyone listened, spellbound, both his men and the country folk who had come to ask him favors."

Castro's energy seemed inexhaustible. Long after his men were asleep, Castro would wake Meneses for one-sided conversations that lasted into the morning hours. He spoke of his dreams for Cuba—all children fed, housed, and educated; medical care for all; all industry owned by the people and used for the good of the people.

"It's a utopia that the rebel chief lays claim to," wrote Meneses, "but it's comforting to know that a person with so much energy and tenacity has such bold ideas for the future."

The future seemed to be drawing closer. Support for the revolution swelled in Cuba among all classes and even among groups with different political beliefs. Powerful businessmen were growing increasingly disgusted with Batista's abuses, and bombs planted by resistance groups exploded regularly in the cities. In March of 1958, the United States suspended arms shipments to Cuba. Batista's brutality had even alienated U.S. officials. He now stood virtually alone.

Anticipating elections scheduled for November, Batista launched an offensive called *Fin de Fidel*—End of Fidel. In May, he sent ten thousand soldiers, supported by tanks and armored cars, into the Sierra Maestra. They had orders to sweep the rebels out of the mountains and into the open plains, where they could be crushed once and for all.

Batista's men were mostly poor and inexperienced, and their overwhelming advantage of numbers was lost in the maze of mountains. They were no match for Castro's veteran fighters. With a superior intelligence network, the rebels cut off and ambushed Batista's columns of soldiers as they approached.

"We have to deal with them with great energy," Castro wrote a friend. "We'll resist on all roads, falling back slowly . . . trying to inflict the greatest number of casualties."

Castro broadcast news of the offensive from a radio transmitter. Government officials noted that more Cubans were buying radio sets in Havana.

On July 11, Castro isolated and surrounded a large force of soldiers. The rebels set up speakers to broadcast appeals for the soldiers to desert their posts and join the rebels. After days of constant harassment, the soldiers realized their situation was hopeless. Castro learned that the army commander was a fellow student from his university days. He proposed a cease-fire, and the army commander quickly surrendered his 146

Some of Castro's soldiers pose on a armored personnel carrier at their base in the Sierra Maestra.

soldiers. Along with the prisoners, the rebels captured two machine guns, a heavy and light mortar, a bazooka (a portable antitank weapon), and ammunition.

The victory was complete, and the disaster demonstrated to the entire country that the offensive had failed. Still, Batista ordered more attacks. On July 30, the rebels captured a tank. In August, torrential downpours soaked the landscape, and Batista's last chance to destroy Castro was drowned in a sea of mud.

By then, Batista's days were numbered. After his spectacular victories, Castro planned to leave the safety of the mountains for the first time and mount an offensive on Havana.

THE REBEL OFFENSIVE

In October, Che Guevara and Camilo Cienfuegos led two groups of troops into the next province, Camagüey. The rebels moved only at night, slipping through swamps and swimming across rivers to secure territory. They harassed any soldiers marching to reinforce the Oriente Province.

On November 20, Castro's army faced its first major test out of the mountains when it surrounded an important army outpost at Guisa. The garrison resisted, with army planes dropping bombs on the rebels when they tried to attack. The rebels used broadcast speakers to insult and mock the soldiers. For ten days, the garrison held out, but when reinforcements did not arrive, the soldiers were forced to retreat. Castro and his men entered the province in triumph.

The rebels began moving north, isolating and overwhelming army posts. The morale of Batista's men plummeted. As Christmas approached, it became clear that Batista was finished. Batista realized it as well. At 3:00 A.M. on January 1, he boarded a plane with his family and flew to the Dominican Republic, never to return to Cuba.

In Havana, excited but fearful crowds filled the streets. Students put up the black and red colors of the 26th of July Movement. As it became clear that Batista was truly gone, the city began celebrating. Parades of motorists eagerly honking their horns crowded intersections. The Cubans also expressed their rage. Houses owned by Batista's supporters were ransacked. Some stores and casinos were looted. But by the end of the day, peace had returned.

On the other side of the island, Castro was preparing to attack the city of Santiago when he heard the news that Batista had fled. Instead of being

Castro speaks to the people of Havana after overthrowing Batista's government.

overjoyed, Castro was angry. "It's a cowardly betrayal! A betrayal!" he cried. "They're trying to steal the triumph that belongs to the revolution!"

Castro promised to continue fighting, but soon there was no one to fight. The commander in Santiago ordered his troops to surrender, and Castro entered the city without firing a shot.

Castro addressed the nation. "Neither crooks, nor traitors, nor interventionists. This time, yes, it is a revolution!"

Across the country, revolutionaries wearing the armbands of the 26th of July Movement took control of local government and police. Castro then began a 600-mile (965.9-km) march to Havana with his victorious army. The march quickly became a parade, as joyful Cubans mobbed the route and cheered. For more than three years, Castro had been a mysterious figure to the Cubans. Now, Cubans had their chance to see the legendary rebel himself. When Castro finally entered Havana on January 8, 1959, hundreds of thousands jammed the streets, stood in windows, and climbed trees to glimpse him as he rode by. Castro was just thirty-two years old.

"The revolution begins now," he told the people of Cuba. "The revolution will not be made in a day, but rest assured, we will make it."

FOUR

Cold War Chess Piece

Castro's speech was heard with a mixture of alarm and curiosity in government circles in Washington, D.C. Who was Castro? What was he going to do? Most important, government officials wondered—was Castro a communist?

Since the end of World War II in 1945, the Soviet Union and the United States had engaged in an increasingly bitter rivalry for world domination that came to be called the Cold War. At first, the United States believed it was winning. After all, the United States enjoyed one of the highest standards of living in the world, far higher than the Soviet Union's.

By the late 1950s, that difference appeared to be vanishing. In October of 1957, the Soviets launched the first satellite, *Sputnik I*, shocking the world and especially the Americans, who had believed their technology to be superior. Nikita Khrushchev, the leader of the Soviet Union, boasted of his country's accomplishments in agriculture and told the people of the West that "we will bury you." In Europe, the countries aligned with the North Atlantic Treaty Organization (NATO), led by the United States, glared across a barbed-wire border at the countries of the Warsaw Pact, led by the Soviet Union.

Communism

The Soviet Union existed under a system called communism, which overlaps with socialism. In broad terms, under communism economy and property are controlled by the state. Everyone works for the common good and each is rewarded according to his or her need, say supporters of communism. What factories produce, and how much they produce, is determined by a central organization. In the Soviet Union, rulers in Moscow planned the economy for the country and heavily influenced the economies in nearby allied countries—East Germany, Hungary, Czechoslovakia, Romania, and Bulgaria.

Communism was a response to the inequalities of capitalism, in which millionaires live in mansions and wield power while their workers toil in factories on barely livable wages.

Some scholars and historians argue that true communism was never actually practiced in the Soviet Union. Castro himself observed in a 1961 interview, "Do not say, however—as Americans do—that there is communism [in Cuba], because communism cannot be found even in Russia, after forty years from the overtaking of power." In any case, it is important to understand that Castro would later use communism—especially its position on private property—for his own purposes.

In those tense times, the Cold War was ready to ignite, and the United States watched Castro nervously. The idea of a communist nation existing in the Western Hemisphere, traditionally an area dominated by the United States, shocked leaders in Washington, D.C.

In the first months after seizing power, however, Castro made few threatening moves. He named Manuel Urrutia president of the new

Castro watches as President Manuel Urrutia signs the document that makes Castro the prime minister. Castro would not share power with Urrutia for very long.

government, and he stated repeatedly that he and his movement were made up of "neither capitalists, nor communists, but humanists."

A series of violent events took place as the young revolutionaries rid Cuba of the former supporters of Batista. Trials began. War criminals were identified and brought to courts, tried, and were usually shot. Some of defendants were guilty of the crimes, but others received punishments that appeared too severe. When forty-three members of the Cuban air force were acquitted of war crimes, Castro stepped in and declared the verdict to be incorrect. Mobilizing public support and appearing in court himself, Castro forced a retrial. The airmen were sentenced to thirty years in prison and ten years of hard labor. Many Cubans who had supported Castro were disturbed. Castro showed that if he didn't agree with the law, the law would have to bend to his wishes.

The wave of trials and executions brought condemnation from around the world. Stung by the criticism, Castro invited foreign journalists to the trials, which were held in stadiums. A poll of the Cuban public showed that 93 percent of the people favored the trials.

In autumn of 1959, Castro turned his attention on Huber Matos, a companion from the days of guerrilla fighting. Matos disagreed with how the revolution was progressing, and Castro felt threatened by his disapproval. Worse, Matos controlled a powerful segment of the Cuban people and commanded loyalty from his troops. To Castro, the situation was intolerable. Matos and thirty-eight of his officers were brought to trial and convicted of treason.

A week after the conviction, Camilo Cienfuegos, a popular revolutionary officer, disappeared in his airplane over the ocean. No one is certain what happened. Three days after his disappearance, Castro ordered a search that found nothing. Apparently, Cienfuegos and Castro had disagreed over the Matos affair. Some Cubans quietly observed a resemblance between Castro's tactics and Batista's.

Castro became prime minister and quickly tired of sharing power with President Urrutia. In his own speeches and proclamations, Castro undercut the power of the new government, which was trying to implement a campaign of reform. No one was sure who was running the country. To make matters more confusing, Castro took a new title, "Maximum Leader."

As a rebel leader hiding in the mountains, Castro had planned a campaign of guerrilla warfare. Now, he was faced with the immense challenges of poverty, unemployment, and an infinite number of other problems. People pestered him day and night, asking questions, seeking advice, and wanting money and jobs.

Castro's own personality did not help bring order to the chaos. He loved to talk to people, and his conversations often rambled for hours and covered several different topics. Castro also addressed thousands of people at a time and expressed his ideas openly. His advisers were unsure if the maximum leader wanted his words implemented as serious law, or whether he was merely thinking out loud.

By 1959, however, the "revolution" Castro had promised the Cuban people had begun to take shape. Supporters of Batista had been executed, imprisoned, or driven from the country. Castro's close followers moved into their giant mansions in Havana and gleefully helped themselves to their automobiles.

On May 17, Castro went to La Plata, one of the scenes of his victories, to introduce a law that confiscated land and distributed it to poor peasants. Any farm larger than 1,000 acres (405 ha) was taken under control of the state. Landowners were reimbursed with guaranteed bonds.

Castro had promised to hold free elections, but now he began to reconsider that plan. Despite being a democracy, the Cuban government had been rife with corruption for decades. Castro considered his own motives to be pure and sincere. He saw himself as the mouthpiece of the Cuban people, of their will, their hopes, and their dreams. As he spoke to the cheering masses in Havana, Castro envisioned a mystical bond between himself and the crowd. Democracy could be bought and sold, but the bond between Castro and his followers could never be broken. Elections, he therefore concluded, were unnecessary.

In those early days, the Cuban people were optimistic. The young revolutionaries, though inexperienced, were hard workers and were not corrupt. "For the first time," said Castro, "there are worthy men at the head of the country who neither sell themselves nor falter nor are intimidated by any threat."

Castro visited the United States in April. Despite tension caused by U.S. criticism, Castro charmed his American hosts, cracking jokes in English and visiting Yankee Stadium and the Bronx Zoo in New York City.

Dressed in olive green army fatigues, sporting a thick beard, and usually smoking a cigar, Castro was a popular figure. A pack of reporters and photographers followed him everywhere. In Washington, D.C., Castro did not meet President Dwight D. Eisenhower, but instead had an interview with Vice President Richard Nixon.

Many Americans asked Castro whether he was a communist.

"Anyone who doesn't sell out or knuckle under is smeared as a communist," he complained. "As for me, I am not selling out to the Americans nor will I take orders from the Americans."

Despite his bold statement, Castro needed help from the United States. In Cuba, unemployment was mounting as economic reforms took hold. Although Castro remained enormously popular, ranchers and landowners attacked him for his seizures of land.

Castro grew increasingly impatient with criticism, especially when he was described as a communist. Urrutia made a speech attacking the Communist Party in Cuba. He hoped to force Castro to make a similar declaration.

Instead, Castro resigned as prime minister on July 17. Castro then made a blistering speech, condemning Urrutia

Castro shakes hands with U.S. Vice President Richard Nixon. He and Nixon talked for more than two hours.

for his anticommunist stance. Cubans jammed the streets, calling for Castro to return to power and Urrutia to resign. Urrutia left Cuba the next day.

Communist influence in Castro's government increased, alarming both Cubans and Americans. The trickle of Cubans leaving the country became a flood. At first, most Cubans had fled because they had connections to Batista, but the latest group was made up of professionals, landowners, laborers, and artists who were growing very worried about Castro's rule. This group of Cuban exiles gathered in Miami and settled in a neighborhood that was soon called "Little Havana." United in their homesickness and their hatred of Castro and communism, they dedicated themselves to overthrowing the "Maximum Leader." They believed their time in Miami would be temporary. Castro would surely be gone within months or, at most, a few years.

Relations between the United States and Cuba quickly soured. Castro seized property held by U.S. companies and citizens, angering the U.S. government. Castro, in turn, was infuriated when airplanes flown by Cuban exiles appeared over Havana and dropped thousands of leaflets accusing Castro of being a communist. The airplanes were flown from airfields in Florida. While the United States did not actively support the propaganda, it did little to stop it.

Castro seethed. In the autumn of 1959, he began openly accusing the United States of deliberately trying to destroy the revolution. When the Cuban exiles began dropping bombs on Cuban cities and fields, Castro's restraint dropped further.

"Put yourself in our place," he demanded. "Suppose planes based in Cuba went over and dropped leaflets or even bombs on Washington.

Suppose we harbored men in our country and had elements in our government who encouraged criminals and revolutionaries plotting to overthrow the United States government? How would you feel? How do you think Cubans feel?"

In Washington, President Eisenhower instructed his ambassadors to tell Castro to tone down his language. In Congress, U.S. leaders threatened to stop buying Cuban sugar.

A TROUBLING ALLIANCE

Castro, however, was already courting another powerful buyer of sugar and potential ally. In February of 1960, the Soviet deputy premier, Anastas Mikoyan, visited Cuba and agreed to a five-year deal to buy Cuban sugar. In April, Soviet oil tankers arrived in Cuba to deliver crude oil to refineries. The refineries, however, were owned by U.S. businesses, and President Eisenhower informed Castro that they were not to be used

Anastas Mikoyan, the Soviet deputy premier (right), talks with Fidel Castro and Ernesto "Che" Guevara in Havana, Cuba.

to process Soviet oil. At the end of June, Castro confiscated all U.S.-owned oil refineries. Soon, all property owned by U.S. citizens on Cuba was seized. Later, U.S. citizens would file insurance claims for lost property that totaled more than $3.3 billion.

President Eisenhower had seen enough. He ordered the Central Intelligence Agency (CIA) to train the anti-Castro Cubans for an invasion of the island. In July, Eisenhower described Cuba as "a nation which has embarked upon a policy of deliberate hostility toward the United States." Privately, he called Castro a "little Hitler." He signed a law curtailing the importation of Cuban sugar. Castro labeled the act a "declaration of economic war."

Rushing to help his new "friend," Soviet Union Premier Khrushchev pledged to buy all Cuban sugar previously purchased by the United States. More menacing, he made a speech challenging the United States's power in the Western Hemisphere.

"Should the need arise, Soviet artillery men can support the Cuban people by missile fire, if the aggressive forces of the Pentagon dare to intervene in Cuba," he said. "The Soviet Union is raising its voice and extends the hand of friendship to the people of Cuba in their fight for independence." To U.S. leaders, a Soviet-Cuban alliance was both terrifying and infuriating.

In September of 1960, Castro and Khrushchev met in New York City at the United Nations (UN). The elderly premier gave the Cuban leader a giant bear hug and grinned widely for the cameras. The new relationship between Cuba and the Soviet Union was reinforced throughout the stay. During one of Khrushchev's speeches at the UN,

Castro leaped up and waved his arms like a cheerleader whenever he or Cuba was mentioned.

When Castro spoke before a packed UN, he began by stating, "Though we have a reputation for speaking at great length, the assembly need not be worried. We shall do our best to be brief."

Speaking to the entire world nearly overwhelmed Castro. He wanted to say everything, and he nearly did. He spoke for four hours—the longest address ever given at the UN.

Castro and Cuba became critically important in the 1960 U.S. presidential election. The Republican nominee, Vice President Richard Nixon, faced John F. Kennedy, who ridiculed the Republicans for allowing communism in Cuba to develop "just eight jet-minutes from Florida."

In reality, the plans for an invasion of Cuba were almost complete, and almost everyone knew it, both in Miami and Havana. In October, the

Castro poses with Nikita Khrushchev, the Soviet premier, in New York City. The Soviet Union would be an important ally for Cuba for many years to come.

United States declared an embargo on Cuba. No trading would take place between the United States and Cuba, except for medicine, medical supplies, and food. The embargo still exists today.

In late November of 1960, Kennedy defeated Nixon by a margin of only a few thousand votes. When Kennedy took office in January, Castro prepared for an imminent invasion.

The CIA continued its preparations, training an assault force of Cuban exiles in the Latin American country of Guatemala. CIA chief Allen Dulles told the new president of the plans. Kennedy was told that at the start, an air attack would destroy Castro's air force. Then as the invasion force swarmed ashore, the Cuban people would revolt against the hated Castro. Castro and his government couldn't survive. Reassured by his advisors, the inexperienced Kennedy gave permission to attack.

A "PERFECT FAILURE"

On April 15, 1961, planes flown by Cuban exiles began bombing the island. The next night, a 1,500-man force left Nicaragua by sea. Its destination was the Bay of Pigs, a landing site on the southern coast of Cuba.

A day later, the ships arrived and the troops swam ashore. Castro was informed of the situation almost immediately. "Forward Cubans!" he announced on the radio. "Answer with steel and with fire the barbarians who despise us and want to make us return to slavery."

Castro ordered his air force to strike the ships still off shore as militia units swung into action. "Tomorrow we are going to shoot down planes, but today we have to sink ships," Castro told Jose Ramon Fernandez, who was in charge of the defenders.

Crippled and without supplies, the invaders were soon trapped on the Cuban beaches. No support was provided to them by the Cuban people, and within one day, the invasion began to collapse. "I think that you have been missing the party," a jubilant Castro told Raúl while the

Castro looks at the wreckage of a U.S. plane after the Bay of Pigs invasion.

fighting raged. Still, the battle was not won and he warned Raúl "you had better be ready."

More than twenty thousand loyal Cuban troops, supported by the Cuban air force, blasted the beachhead. In Washington, D.C., President Kennedy watched the disaster unfold with horror, but he did not commit U.S. troops to help the trapped rebel forces. On April 18, Castro's troops wiped out the invasion force, capturing 1,189 and killing more than one hundred rebels.

For the United States, the defeat was total. One person called it "a perfect failure." Castro's reputation, both home and abroad, soared to new heights. The revolution had faced its hardest test and triumphed, and Castro savored the victory. The United States, a tyrannical giant, had been humiliated and was forced to pay $53 million worth of supplies and food for the return of the rebels.

After the disaster, the CIA, under intense pressure, desperately concocted fantastic and absurd schemes to get rid of Castro, whom they

The Beard

According to Tad Szulc, the author of a biography on Castro, Castro has made the beard his symbol. With his typical obsession with details, Castro calculated that it took fifteen minutes a day to shave. That's five thousand minutes a year, time better spent reading, studying, or exercising. Castro also has made sure that no one in his circle grows a beard that is thicker and healthier than his. He has ordered his closest associates to remain freshly shaven. At most, they have worn mustaches.

nicknamed "the beard." One plan was to poison Castro's cigars. Another plan called for putting special chemicals in his shoes that would make his hair fall out. Without his beard, thought some in the CIA, Castro's magnetic power over the Cuban people would be gone. The most flawed plan involved the CIA turning to organized criminals in the United States and trying to hire an assassin to kill Castro.

TO THE BRINK OF NUCLEAR WAR

One of the consequences of the invasion of Cuba and the CIA tactics was an increase of arms shipments to Cuba from the Soviet Union. Castro was convinced that the failure at the Bay of Pigs would be followed by a stronger invasion, this time by U.S. Marines. Khrushchev, determined to extend his power into the Western Hemisphere, offered Cuba the protection of Soviet nuclear missiles. Soviet freighters began

This is a U.S. Department of Defense photograph that shows Soviet missile equipment being loaded at the Mariel naval port in Cuba.

In a nationally televised speech, U.S. President John F. Kennedy says that there will be war if the missiles are not removed from Cuba.

arriving in Havana with secret cargoes that were transported in boxes to hastily constructed missile sites.

Both Castro and Khrushchev thought the presence of nuclear missiles in Cuba would be firm security against an invasion. U.S. spy planes took photographs of the sites that were developed within hours and shown to President Kennedy. Shocked, Kennedy contemplated that a Soviet nuclear bomb was just minutes away from the U.S. border. It was too much.

On October 22, 1962, President Kennedy appeared on television and told the nation that the Soviets had committed an unacceptable act of aggression. Unless the missiles were immediately withdrawn under UN supervision, said Kennedy, there would be war. U.S. troops were ordered to assemble in Florida, and Kennedy ordered the navy to place Cuba under a blockade. All ships going to Cuba would be searched, and only those with non-military cargoes would be permitted to go through.

For the next seven days, the world watched as the Soviet Union and the United States drifted toward nuclear war. At first, Khrushchev denied doing anything wrong, roared his disapproval of the blockade, and promised Castro he would protect him.

Khrushchev, however, had misjudged the situation, and he knew it. After days of sending letters and messages, Khrushchev offered to withdraw the missiles if the United States agreed not to invade Cuba. Kennedy accepted, and the world sighed with relief.

Castro, however, was infuriated. It was obvious that his nation was just a pawn being manipulated by the two superpowers. In the next eight years, Castro would strive to demonstrate that his own brand of socialism could succeed and that Cuba could determine its own foreign policy.

FIVE

The Cuban
Socialist Experiment

In an attempt to increase Cuba's influence in the world, Castro began supporting communist revolutionaries in other parts of Latin America, despite Soviet disapproval. Cuba, said Castro, is "a small country with a large country's foreign policy."

In Cuba, the wrenching changes in the economy and social order produced a wave of discontent. Thousands of Cubans, especially the wealthy and professional, fled the island and were labeled "worms" by the Cuban government. The resentment, however, rarely threatened Castro's power. Any person who dared to protest ended up in jail.

The government declared 1961 to be the "Year of Education," and more than 100,000 secondary school students journeyed to the countryside to teach illiterate peasants to read. After a year, 700,000 adults had learned some basic reading skills.

Castro began reforming the economy, especially the country's dependence on sugar. Energetic, passionate, and convinced of the infallibility of his own plans, Castro paid attention to every detail. When the government began building housing projects, he selected the furnishings in the kitchens and the bedrooms and the paint color for the walls. Consequently, Castro spent much of his time racing around the island in his jeep, doing work that would probably have better been handled by lesser administrators.

Castro's attempt to diversify Cuba's agriculture proved disastrous. In an attempt to reduce Cuba's reliance on sugar, Castro ordered farmers to plant a variety of crops. Confused and inexperienced, farmers plowed under fields best suited for sugarcane and replaced them with crops they

Students gather to celebrate the fortieth anniversary of the "Year of Education" in Havana in 2001.

did not know how to cultivate. By 1964, Castro conceded defeat and switched the country back to the production of sugar.

THE "NEW MAN"

The Cuban revolution soon faced another problem. In communist theory, workers are supposed to labor for the common good, not for personal profit or gain. By producing more, a worker earns the cherished satisfaction of having contributed to the success of the revolution.

But this theory worked only in theory. Despite constant urging in speeches and the press, many workers loafed or faked illness to escape the drudgery of their jobs. Those who worked hard resented those who didn't.

Che Guevara proposed a model of a "new man" for Cuba—one who was imbued with the revolutionary spirit and loved to labor. But Castro was more realistic and established a system that gave bonuses to those who worked harder. In January of 1965, the Cuban government awarded one thousand East German motorcycles, fifteen hundred refrigerators, and two thousand beach vacations to the best workers. Despite the setbacks, Castro was convinced that the revolution would change Cuba into a paradise by 1970.

SPREADING THE REVOLUTION

As Castro carried out his reforms, hostility between the United States and the island nation worsened. The CIA attempted several times to assassinate Castro. In 1964, the United States asked other Latin American countries to break off diplomatic contact with the Cubans. Every country except Mexico agreed.

The Cubans further increased tensions when they began to send troops and advisers to Africa and Latin America, where the United States and Soviet Union were engaged in a delicate but deadly bid for influence. Cuba's presence was not welcomed by either side.

In 1967, Guevara traveled secretly to Bolivia, where he tried to repeat the success he and Castro had achieved in Cuba. The Bolivian peasants were in no mood to revolt, and the CIA trained hundreds of Bolivians in anti-guerrilla techniques. Lacking supplies, Guevara and his ragged band fled into the mountains, but were finally captured in October of 1967. The Bolivian soldiers executed Guevara soon afterward. When Castro heard the news, he reportedly went to his room and expressed his grief by punching and kicking the doors, walls, and furniture.

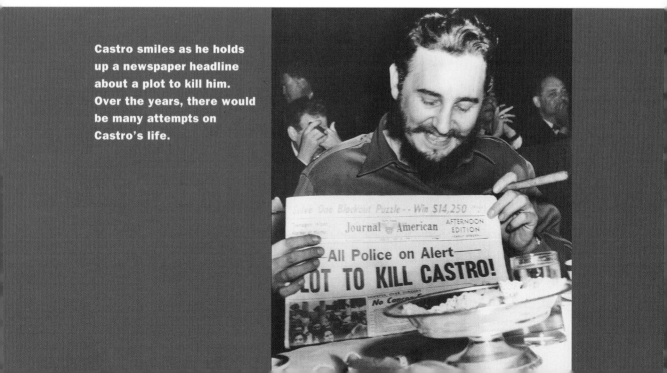

Castro smiles as he holds up a newspaper headline about a plot to kill him. Over the years, there would be many attempts on Castro's life.

"Che was one of the most extraordinary examples known to history of fidelity to revolutionary principals, of integrity, of valor, of generosity and unselfishness," Castro said at Guevara's funeral address. Cuba entered three days of national mourning, and October 8 was declared Day of the Heroic Guerrilla Fighter.

Later, many historians questioned Castro's demonstrations of pain. Cuban supplies never seemed to get to Guevara in Bolivia, and messages between Havana and the embattled guerrilla ceased in the weeks before Guevara was killed. In the end, Guevara was left alone. Guevara's death was a serious setback for Castro's plan to export his revolution outside Cuba's borders. It clearly demonstrated that similar guerrilla movements in other Latin American countries had little chance of success.

The Soviet Union, which had watched Castro's foreign policy with growing disapproval, wanted Castro to be more in line with the goals of its foreign policy. As the economy expanded, Cuba's need for oil also

Cuba mourned the death of one of its revolutionaries, Ernesto "Che" Guevara.

increased. By 1966, reserves were low and Castro requested 8 percent more fuel from the Soviet Union. Moscow replied by increasing the fuel exports to Cuba a meager 2 percent. The negotiations between the countries broke down.

By 1968, Cuba was having a serious energy crisis, and Castro was forced to ration gasoline. Instead of giving in, Castro chided the Soviet Union publicly for failing to deliver oil on time. In private, he was even less patient. "The Soviet Union really has no moral right to insist on her contractual rights and the superhuman sacrifices these entail for Cuba," he complained to a Polish socialist. "They give us nothing for nothing, and then they act as though they were showering us with gold."

Lack of oil wasn't the only scarcity plaguing Cuba. Food from the United States was no longer available, and Cuba was forced to export much of its own food to pay debts. Still, no peasant starved, and improved access to health care was reducing the infant mortality rate.

In March of 1968, Castro had to announce that the milk ration would be cut off for adults. In a speech that lasted six hours, Castro consulted reams of statistics to explain the latest deprivation. Then, in a bold turn, Castro described a radical solution to the ills still hindering the full development of the revolution—terminate all private business.

Large corporations had been confiscated by the government long before, but Castro had allowed small store owners to remain in business. At this point, Castro changed his mind and focused his attention on confiscating the businesses of bar owners, whom he described as merciless people who profited off the misery of others. He did not stop at bars. Auto repair shops, beauty salons, laundries, hardware stores, dry cleaners—more than 55,000 in all—were stormed by revolution supporters and shuttered for good.

These small stores, essential for the quality of life of Cubans, were replaced with stores run by the state. The employees received the same wage, regardless of how many people they served or the amount of goods they provided. Frustration swelled in Cuba, and anti-Castro graffiti began appearing on the walls of buildings in the cities. Some Cubans derisively called him "Mr. There-Will-Be," since all Castro seemed able to talk about was the future. In more extreme acts of defiance, Cubans sabotaged warehouses and schools. The press, however, had long been censored by Castro, and no open dissent appeared in print.

Artists and Castro

In Castro's Cuba, speaking or writing words that criticized Castro was considered "counterrevolutionary" and could land a person in jail. Castro was particularly sensitive to what intellectuals—writers, thinkers, and artists—said. When news spread that Castro ruled Cuba harshly, he angrily blamed the intellectuals for spreading the information. Many were taken to prison and forced to confess that they had tried to destroy the revolution. One poet, Herberto Padilla, was arrested and interrogated. He then delivered a speech praising Castro and blasting other intellectuals for not supporting him. Padilla's words caused a harsh reaction in Europe and the United States. Many important artists outside Cuba no longer supported the Cuban revolution.

Castro acted more repressively than the regime he overthrew. He could not stand criticism. While Cubans who committed crimes could expect fair treatment in court, they could expect little consideration if their offense was against the political order. Cubans were seized and

The Cuban people worked hard to meet Castro's sugar quota, but were unable to reach his goal.

taken to jails, where they languished without lawyers or court dates. Castro's political prisoners have never been counted, but some observers have estimated the number to be in the thousands.

The wave of national resentment came at a bad time for Castro. For years, he had told the Cuban people that the 1970 sugarcane harvest would be the greatest in history—10 million tons. Nothing would be spared from the effort. To fail, said Castro, would be a crushing blow and a national humiliation.

Castro mobilized the Cuban population for the effort as if he were fighting a war. A million workers were diverted from their jobs and sent into the fields with machetes. More than 100,000 soldiers followed.

By May, the harvest was at 7.7 million tons. The Cubans worked harder, but the quotas were too high. At the end of the harvest, 8.5 million tons of sugarcane were collected, more than during any other harvest in Cuba's history, but not achieving Castro's cherished 10 million tons.

"Never again, I hope, shall I have to carry out the bitter task of breaking such news," he said. In an emotional speech, Castro told the people he would resign. They chanted "no." Castro, of course, agreed with the will of the people.

Castro had to admit a greater defeat than just the failure to meet his ambitious sugar quota. Cuba's efficiency was getting worse as more and more workers produced less and less. An anti-loafing law was passed, but nothing seemed to help. Castro realized that the revolution, his revolution, was not going as planned and would need to be reformed.

Castro delivers a speech in the 1970s, a time when his government would experience some challenges.

SIX

The Mariel Boatlift

Cuba's failure to produce 10 million tons of sugar helped convince Castro that Soviet socialism offered the best solution for achieving economic and social success. Cuban-Soviet relations warmed, aid increased, and the Soviet Union deferred payment of Cuban loans into the 1990s. Castro also gained admission to the Organization of American States. The United States maintained its embargo, but both countries began to establish contacts to break their long-standing quarrel.

As the diplomats negotiated, Castro and U.S. President Gerald Ford showed no signs of compromising. Especially troubling to the United States was the presence of Cuban soldiers in the African nation of Angola to support communist forces waging a civil war. Castro argued that he had the right to aid revolutionary forces anywhere in the world. The United States demanded that Castro stop exporting his revolution and that he compensate citizens for property his government had seized. Castro angrily rejected these conditions, called for the end of the embargo, and refused to negotiate further. In 1976, the U.S. State Department canceled a goodwill baseball game between all-stars from Cuba and the United States. The brief window of opportunity for a better relationship between the two nations closed.

The Cuban economy struggled as sugar prices remained low, and Castro acknowledged that times were difficult.

"We are sailing on a sea of difficulties, have been sailing for a long time. And we shall continue on this sea, sometimes stormy, at other times more calm, toward the distant shore. We shall not soon cross it," he said.

The "First Lady" of Cuba

Castro never remarried after his divorce, but he did have many female companions. One, named Celia Sánchez, was Castro's devoted adviser and supporter from the times of the revolution. In her apartment in Havana, Castro could relax, converse, and enjoy her cooking. Sánchez was one of the few people in the world who could tell Castro directly when he was wrong. Because of her closeness to Castro, Sánchez had a high position in the government, exercised great power, and was regarded as the "first lady" of Cuba. After her death from cancer in 1980, Castro had her street cordoned off by guards, and the apartment was kept for him to visit.

THE MARIEL BOATLIFT

After thirty years, the Cuban people were tired of waiting for the success of the revolution. Their desire to escape Castro's rule became desperate. In Havana, Cubans crashed their cars through the gates of foreign embassies and begged for asylum. Castro responded by posting armed guards at the embassies.

In April of 1980, six Cubans stole a bus and rammed it into the Peruvian Embassy. The guards shot at the bus, killing one of their own comrades in the crossfire. The fleeing Cubans escaped. When Castro heard the news, he exploded in a fit of anger. The slain guard was honored as a hero of the revolution, and Castro withdrew all soldiers from the

Not everyone supported the Cubans who sought asylum at the embassy. Cuban protestors hold a sign comparing the Peruvian Embassy to a waste disposal site.

embassies. Castro expected that the ambassadors would then take security precautions of their own to prevent Cubans from fleeing the country.

However, something completely different happened. When Cubans heard that the embassies were left open, many packed their bags and sought asylum in them. By April 6, more than ten thousand Cubans, sick and tired of Castro's regime, crowded onto the Peruvian Embassy grounds. They occupied the rooms and halls of the buildings, packed into the courtyards, climbed trees, and sat on the roof.

Castro, shocked by the response, blamed U.S. imperialism and culture for corrupting thousands of the country's citizens. The communist newspaper labeled the refugees as misfits, lunatics, and drug abusers who could not stand the rigors of socialism.

The reality was different. One woman told a reporter that she had gotten married, but could not get a house. Her husband and two children lived in the same cramped room she had occupied when single. Her entire family had decided to flee to seek a better life.

Because the people wanted to leave, Castro decided to let them. The United States and other Latin American countries agreed to take refugees. Airplanes roared back and forth between Havana and Miami. However, Castro ended the airlift after just two days. Predicting that he could halt the embarrassing flight of his people, he invited the Cuban exiles in Florida to use their ships to ferry refugees from Cuba to the United States.

Once again, Castro had miscalculated. Boats and ships, large and small, of every kind and description, showed up in the Cuban port of Mariel. Thousands of refugees jammed onto the vessels for the trip to Florida and a new life. In a single day, more than six hundred ships made the journey.

At first, President Jimmy Carter welcomed the new Cuban refugees. "Ours is a country of refugees," he said. "We'll continue to provide an open heart and open arms to refugees seeking freedom from communist domination."

They kept coming. Every day, thousands more, many clutching their sole possessions or carrying them on their backs, dared the passage.

This photograph shows one of the many ships used to transport Cubans to the United States.

Castro, who now realized how bad the situation was, deftly turned it to his advantage. He emptied Cuba's prisons and mental institutions and gleefully sent the former inmates to Florida.

"They are doing an excellent sanitation job for us. The best," jeered Castro in a speech. He noted that the United States government had realized that criminals were among the refugees. "Now [the Americans] are complaining. They say there are delinquents. As if this was a great discovery. As if they were amazed to find some delinquents. Now, who do they think broke into and took refuge in the Peruvian Embassy? Did they think they were intellectuals, artists, technicians, engineers?"

Now President Carter looked foolish. He ordered the U.S. Coast Guard to halt the ships and arrest their captains, but the refugees continued to come.

When the boatlift finally came to an end, more than 100,000 Cubans had fled the country. Castro proclaimed that Cuba had finally rid itself of useless slackers, called lumpen, who had kept the country from succeeding. Carter had appeared weak and inept as he handled the crisis. Later, he attributed the Mariel Boatlift as a major cause of his defeat in the November 1980 presidential election to Ronald Reagan.

THE COLD WAR RENEWED

When President Reagan took office, relations with Cuba entered a new, frigid phase. Reagan was a vocal anticommunist who spoke of creating a new Monroe Doctrine. He increased spending on the military by billions of dollars. In Cuba, Castro compared Reagan to Hitler and increased the size of his army.

Reagan and Castro hurled insults at each other. One White House spokesperson suggested that Castro needed to have his mouth taped shut. When Castro observed an outbreak of fever in Cuba, he blamed it on the CIA.

The U.S. State Department forbade U.S. tourists from visiting the island. "There is a lot more we can to do to hurt the Cubans, and we are seriously considering all the options," said a Reagan spokesman.

On a Caribbean island called Grenada, Cuban and Soviet engineers and soldiers helped in the construction of a giant runway. When Grenada experienced a violent coup in October of 1983, Reagan sent in thousands of soldiers to seize the island.

Reagan, and most of the United States, was thrilled. "There was no way this administration was going to miss the chance to kick Fidel where it hurts and take one back from the communists," said an aide.

Castro called the invasion a "brutal violation." "Where is the glory, the greatness, the victory in invading and conquering one of the smallest countries in the world, with no economic or strategic significance?" he

An End to Smoking

In 1985, Castro shocked the smoking world when he suddenly decided to give up his beloved cigars. He called it a "last sacrifice" as part of a health campaign to get Cubans to stop smoking. "If someone had forced me to quit, I would have suffered," Castro told biographer Tad Szulc. "But since I forced myself to halt smoking, without any solemn promise, it worked."

asked. "Where is the heroism of fighting against a handful of Cuban workers and civilian technicians?"

As the Cold War heated up, Castro dealt with the annual issue of the sugar harvest. Rainy weather had seriously damaged crops, and in 1985, Castro was again stressing the need for hard work and efficiency.

"Who is the genius who invented the coffee break?" he complained to a reporter from *The New York Times*. The sugar harvest had taken on a disturbing pattern. At the beginning of the season, Castro would ask the Cuban people to produce an unreasonable amount of sugar. At the end of the season, he spent his time explaining why the goal had not been met.

While Castro continuously tried to make his revolution successful, change was sweeping through the world. These changes were so radical, so sudden, and so shocking that the Cold War would come to an end, not in nuclear war, but in a peaceful way. The changes would leave Cuba and Castro suddenly alone.

SEVEN

Gorbachev, the Pope, and a Boy Named Elián

The changes began with a new Soviet premier—Mikhail Gorbachev. Young and dynamic, Gorbachev was determined to deal openly with a host of problems facing communist nations around the world. These problems included repressive governments and economies that were on the verge of collapse.

During the early 1980s, President Reagan had escalated the arms race by building up the size and strength of the U.S. military. The Soviets watched in alarm and tried to keep pace, but they could not. Their economy, weaker and smaller, strained under the demands. By the time

Mikhail Gorbachev led a series of reforms that brought about the end of the Soviet Union.

Gorbachev took power, he acknowledged that communism had to change. He called his new approach *glasnost*, meaning "openness."

Gorbachev could blame former Soviet leaders for the country's problems, but who could Castro blame? He was the revolution, its sole leader, and its strongest supporter. To condemn the revolution or communism in Cuba was to condemn Castro, and that was dangerous.

Castro watched the changes taking place in the Soviet Union with increasing discomfort. In 1988, he proclaimed that Cuba would stand guard over the purity of the revolution. He openly criticized Gorbachev, but by that time, no one noticed. The world was changing at a rate beyond Castro's and most everyone's grasp.

A NEW WORLD

Soviet communism was collapsing. In 1990, the Soviet Union held its first open elections since 1918, and Russian

Boris Yeltsin received 90 percent of the vote. In Eastern Europe, Poland, Czechoslovakia, and Hungary rose up against their communist governments. When the Soviets indicated that they would not intervene, the Berlin Wall dividing East and West Germany came tumbling down.

After costing billions of dollars, destroying millions of lives, and causing forty years of deadly rivalry, the Cold War was over. In Cuba, Castro vowed to fight on. "Long live rigidity!" he exclaimed. "We don't care who or what falls from power anywhere, but here nothing is going to fall!"

Then came another blow: the disintegration of the Soviet Union. Suddenly, the billions of dollars in aid and oil that were delivered every year to Cuba were no longer available. Castro urged the people of Cuba to make even greater sacrifices.

In Miami, eager Cuban exiles prepared lists of the property they would reclaim after Castro fell. In Washington, President George Bush

Because of the loss of support from the Soviets, the Cuban people had to cope with more hardship. They would often have to wait in long lines to get basic necessities, such as food.

told a group of exiles that he looked forward to walking down the streets of a free Havana.

Many Cubans began making desperate trips on rafts and boats, hoping to travel safely across the 90 miles (144.8 km) separating Florida and Cuba. A crisis erupted in January of 1996, when two civilian aircraft flown by an anti-Castro group based in Florida were shot down by Cuban fighter jets in international airspace. The anti-Castro group that made the flights was called "Brothers to the Rescue." Since 1992, the organization had flown over the waters between Cuba and Florida, searching for Cubans who had fled the island on makeshift rafts and needed help. Castro claimed that the airplanes had been shot down in Cuban airspace. Secretary of State Madeleine Albright said that Brothers to the Rescue had probably flown into or very near Cuban airspace on a number of occasions. But she also noted that the Soviet Union, even at the height of the Cold War, had not shot down unarmed

Pope John Paul II visited Cuba in January and conducted several outdoor masses for the people of Cuba.

planes in international airspace. President Bill Clinton and Congress responded to the uproar by tightening the embargo.

In January of 1998, Pope John Paul II visited the island nation, where he was welcomed by cheering crowds. Under Castro, the Catholic Church's schools had been taken over and the official religion declared "atheist." As a gesture to the Pope, Castro allowed Cubans to celebrate Christmas for the first time in decades and freed three hundred political prisoners. The Pope criticized the U.S. embargo, but also urged Cubans to become more religious.

The Pope had played a significant role in toppling communism in Eastern Europe, and many expected that his visit would cause a similar outcome in Cuba. In a speech delivered before hundreds of thousands of people in Havana, the Pope called for Castro's government to respect the rights of the individual. The anti-Castro cries of *Libertad!*, or freedom or liberty, were heard from the crowd, a chant that hadn't been heard in nearly forty years. The media was filled with columns and articles that predicted Castro's fall and what Cuba would be like once he was gone. *Harper's Magazine* published an article titled "Hasta La Vista, Fidel." In 1999, U.S government representatives announced that fifteen thousand immigration visas to the United States would be awarded through a lottery. More than 500,000 people applied.

Still, somehow, Castro held onto power. With the Cold War over, world leaders criticized the United States for enforcing a cruel embargo that seemed to punish Cuba's people more than its leaders. The exiles in Miami, who longed for their return to Cuba, had become a powerful force in Florida politics. Anyone wishing to become president would not willingly alienate these important voters.

If Castro was out of place in a world that had passed him by, so were the exiles in their adopted country, the United States. This was clearly demonstrated in a case of a young Cuban boy named Elián Gonzalez.

ELIÁN GONZALEZ

On November 21, 1999, fourteen Cubans seeking asylum in the United States piloted a ship toward Florida. The craft capsized, drowning eleven of them. The remaining three, including an exhausted five-year-old boy named Elián Gonzalez, were picked up by two Florida fishermen.

Elián's mother and stepfather were among those drowned, and relatives of the boy quickly took him into their custody in a home in the Little Havana neighborhood of Miami. "God wanted him here for freedom," cousin Marilysis Gonzalez said. "And he's here, and he will get it."

Elián's father, divorced from his mother, still lived in Cuba. Castro demanded that the Miami relatives return the boy. "We will move heaven and earth to get the child back!" he cried. "If they have any brains, they will make sure the boy is returned within 72 hours." Cuban citizens crowded into the streets of Havana and staged mass demonstrations. Elián's father asked Castro to help him retrieve his son.

In Miami, the Cuban exiles refused to allow Elián return to what they called "hell."

Castro accused the United States of kidnapping Elián. Usually, in international custody cases, a child would be quickly returned to his or her parent. But the boy had become a symbol of the rage between the Cuban exiles and Castro. To the exiles, Elián represented the extraordinary pain of their lives away from Cuba and their hatred for the dictator who ruled it. Castro's angry demands from Havana only hardened attitudes throughout Miami. For them, to give Elián up became an act akin to surrendering to evil.

Demonstrators march down Malecon Avenue in Havana, heading to a demonstration asking for the return of Elián Gonzalez.

"I think that you must understand the Elián case as a metaphor," Damian Fernandez, chairman of the International Relations Department at Florida International University, told a PBS interviewer. "And both sides, here in Miami and there in Havana and throughout Cuba, they were fighting for the nation of tomorrow."

The dispute soon worsened. A congressman sponsored a bill to have Elián declared a U.S. citizen. Millions of Cubans marched in Havana, pumping their fists in the air and chanting "We want Elián!" In Florida, many in the community of exiles spoke of Elián's survival as a miracle of God. Elián's relatives took him to see Disney World.

The U.S. Immigration and Naturalization Service (INS) finally ordered that the boy be returned to his father. Elián's relatives filed a request in a Florida court to be appointed his legal guardians. The court defied the INS and ordered Elián to remain in the United States until March, when the court would decide to award or deny his relatives temporary custody. The Miami mayor pledged that city police would not help INS agents take Elián back to Cuba. People across the nation wondered aloud if Miami thought it was a separate country.

"You know, you come over here and you want to be an American, but you don't want to go by our laws," an angry demonstrator told a crowd of Elián supporters in Miami.

Again, Castro and the Cuban people raged. The Miami exiles fumed, stating that Elián's mother had died to give him freedom. The INS came under criticism for deporting Haitians and other seekers of political asylum without a pause. Why hesitate when dealing with a Cuban boy?

Finally, Attorney General Janet Reno ordered that the case of Elián's custody be decided in a federal court. The federal court negated the Florida court's decision. Still, many of the people of "Little Havana" refused to back down. The Miami relatives vowed not to give Elián up, saying that he preferred Miami to Cuba. They formed a human chain around the home where Elián was staying and dared the federal government to come and take him.

On April 6, Elián's father, Juan-Miguel, arrived in Washington, D.C., to take personal custody of his son. In "Little Havana," the mood grew frantic. The Miami mayor said that any violence that occurred over Elián was the responsibility of the federal government, and especially of Reno.

Reno gave the order to return Elián to Cuba. "This is a nation of laws by which all must abide," said Reno. "There is a bond, a special, wonderful, sacred bond between a father and his son, one that I intend to uphold." At 5:14 A.M., on the morning of April 24, gun-wielding federal agents stormed the house. They seized Elián and reunited him hours later with his father.

The battle wasn't over. The Cuban exiles protested bitterly and organized demonstrations. They made offers to Juan-Miguel, saying he could stay in Miami and live a comfortable life with Elián. Juan-Miguel, however, refused. After two months, on June 28, Elián and his father stepped off a plane in Cuba. Castro was there to greet him. Castro awarded Juan-Miguel a medal of honor for courage.

"I have done nothing that any father who loved his son and believed in socialism and the revolution would not have done," said

Juan-Miguel. Castro, who must have especially liked the last comment, had triumphed again.

Castro also appeared delighted with U.S. opinion polls that overwhelmingly supported the return of Elián to his father. In September of 2000, Castro spoke at Riverside Church in New York City, telling the crowd that Elián was back in school and doing well. "Our people will never forget and will always thank the American people who spoke out en masse in favor of the legitimate rights of a father and his son," he said. "Once more I said to myself: the American people are very idealistic, therefore, for them to support an unjust cause they first have to be deceived."

The Cuban American Community

About 700,000 Cuban Americans live in and around Miami. Since fleeing Cuba, they have formed a powerful and influential community that has maintained its culture and identity. Many await the day Castro's regime ends.

"As a community, we came here and we very much made a decision that we were not going to integrate into the mainstream of American society, in the sense that other immigrant groups have done before," Carlos Saldrigas, a Florida businessman, told a PBS reporter. "We didn't come here with a specific desire to become a part of the melting pot."

THE COLD WAR LIVES ON

The Elián Gonzalez situation proved that the Cold War might have been dead in most of the world, but it lived on in Cuba and in Miami. Most Americans supported the return of Elián and newspaper editorials severely criticized the Miami community of exiles for separating a boy and his father. The rest of the world had moved on. When China, also a Communist nation where one party has ruled for decades, was granted most favored nation status by Congress in May of 2000, some U.S. leaders, especially from farm states, wondered why Cuba was still not allowed to engage in free trade.

Elián Gonzalez arrives back in Cuba with his father, stepmother, and half-brother.

EIGHT

A Contested Legacy

In October of 2002, a U.S. company sold something directly to Cuba that hadn't been seen in Cuba since 1959—Wrigley's chewing gum. The trade was made possible by a law passed in 2000 that allowed U.S. companies to sell food directly to Cuba, as long as the Cubans paid in cash. By 2001, Castro signed a $10 million contract with ADM, a large American food company, for rice, soy beans, and cooking oil. It was the first time a U.S. company had sold food formally to Cuba in forty years. In 2002, Cuba ranked forty-fifth in countries that purchase food from the United States, up from 228th in 2001. In 2003, Cuba is expected to spend $200 million on American farm products.

The changes reflect a new reality in Cuba, even if Castro still keeps his grip on power. To attract more money to Cuba, Castro has allowed use of the U.S. dollar and has ambitiously campaigned to bring foreign tourists to the island. These visitors gawk at a world that seems partially frozen in time, where American cars from the 1950s are still driven through Havana boulevards, which are lined with crumbling grand buildings. The life of Cubans, however, goes on.

"Every doorway, however, teems with human life; every window frames a face or cluster of faces, every other hallway broadcasts the libidinous pounding of salsa on to the street," wrote a journalist in the British newspaper *The Observer*. "Women carry their loads, girls display their

Jimmy Carter and his wife Rosalyn walk with Castro in Havana. During his visit, Carter told the Cuban people that they have the right to democracy and freedom. Carter also called for an end to the U.S. ban on travel to and on trade with Cuba.

velvet skin; men gather on corners to chat, boys strut their muscles; the bright fluorescent lights of cafes and bars illuminate noisy card games."

On May 5, 2002, former President Jimmy Carter visited Cuba. Carter had blamed the Mariel Boatlift as a major reason that he failed to be reelected. After his term as president, Carter dedicated himself to humanitarian causes and had won worldwide recognition for his efforts on behalf of peace. The visit to Castro was another such effort. In Cuba, Carter was allowed to visit with opponents of Castro. He toured factories. Speaking in Spanish, Carter gave an unedited speech that was broadcast to the Cuban people. It summarized the distrust between the two nations, called for an end to the embargo, and voiced the hope that Cuba would embrace democracy. "Our two nations have been trapped in a destructive state of belligerence for forty-two years, and it is time for us to change our relationship and the way we think and talk about each other," he said. "Because the United States is the most powerful nation, we should take the first step."

Carter called for the United States to repeal the embargo and permit unrestricted travel to and from Cuba. He also addressed the anger and needs of the Cuban exile community in southern Florida, which he said should be integrated into future plans for the island.

"Are such normal relationships possible?" Carter asked. "I believe they are." Carter also criticized Castro. He noted that except for the tense relationship between the United States and Cuba, the rest of the world had moved on. South America, which had once been ruled by dictators, had become a continent of democracies. Cuba, Carter noted, was a government in which only one party ruled and the people had no opportunity to vote for a change.

"Your constitution recognizes freedom of speech and association, but other laws deny these freedoms to those who disagree with the government," said Carter. Carter noted that eleven thousand Cubans had signed a petition asking for multiparty elections and other freedoms, including freedom of the press. According to the Cuban constitution, the government must consider a petition signed by ten thousand people. Carter's verbal gesture seemed a sign of hope that Cuba's people could one day rule themselves.

"After forty-three years of animosity," Carter said in his conclusion, "We hope that someday soon, you can reach across the great divide that separates our two countries and say, 'We are ready to join the community of democracies,' and I hope that Americans will soon open our arms to you and say, 'We welcome you as our friends.'"

The reaction to Carter's speech ranged from glowing to furious. The speech made little impact in Washington, D.C., where President George W. Bush said that the embargo would stay in place until Castro had demonstrated that he would truly reform.

Jorge Mas Santos, chairman of the anti-Castro Cuban American National Foundation, discussed the speech on PBS's *NewsHour* with Jim Lehrer. Mas Santos praised Carter for speaking to the Cubans openly about human rights and democracy, but he did not want the embargo lifted.

"I want to point out that there is really no problem between the people of the United States and the people of Cuba," said Mas Santos. "What keeps the United States from having normal relations with Cuba is Castro, who is the worst violator of human rights this hemisphere has ever seen."

LEGACY OF A CONTROVERSIAL LEADER

Trying to determine Castro's legacy is as difficult as predicting when he will leave power. Castro can boast about the many accomplishments of the revolution, despite his dictatorship, the embargo, and the open hostility of the most powerful country in the world. The Cubans suffer from shortages of food and modern conveniences, but few starve. The Cuban

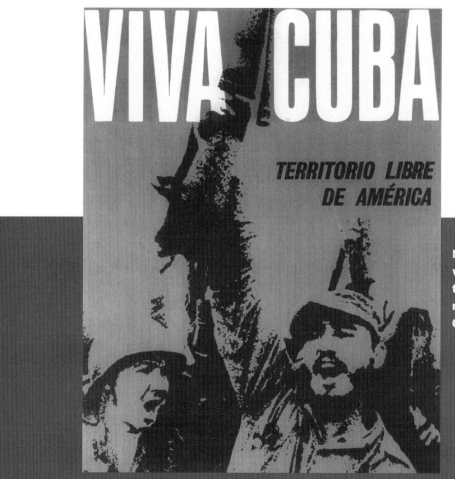

Many people wonder what will happen to the revolutionary movement after Castro is gone.

healthcare system had lowered the infant mortality rate to about sixteen deaths per one thousand births—a rate that rivals that of the United States and Europe. Life expectancy had ballooned from 57 years in 1958 to 73.5 years in the mid-1980s. Education is available to most, if not all, of the population.

There is the other side of Castro's revolution, however. For more than forty years, he has held tightly to power, allowing no challengers or dissent. He has jailed and executed thousands of people for resisting his rule or for living a lifestyle he condemns. His harsh policies and version of socialism has seized property and fortunes. Hundreds of thousands have been forced to flee their homes, many trying to brave the passage to the United States by clinging to rafts. Many have not survived.

In April 2003, Castro showed that he had no intention of releasing his tyrannical grip on power. Three men who hijacked a ferry and tried to steer it to the United States were executed by firing squad. Castro also ordered a crackdown on opponents of his regime. Almost eighty people were arrested and sentenced to long prison terms. Castro's actions drew condemnation from around the world.

History, it is safe to say, will remember both sides of Fidel Castro's rule. Although he has confounded those who predicted his fall, Castro will eventually lose power. Then the question will become who will rule Cuba and how. Castro's influence and the impact of his personality will certainly influence those decisions, and long after he is gone the chants of "Fidel!" will live on in Cuban history, a symbol of both inspiration and tyranny.

Timeline

Timeline

1962 The Cuban Missile Crisis takes place in October. The world teeters on the edge of nuclear war.

1967 Ernesto "Che" Guevara is executed in Bolivia on October 9.

1970 Castro's goal of producing 10 million tons of sugar fails.

1980 Castro allows more than 100,000 Cubans, some of them mental patients and prisoners, to flee the country for the United States in April.

1991 The Soviet Union collapses.

Castro loses subsidies for Cuba from the Soviet Union.

1998 Castro allows Pope John Paul II to visit Cuba and perform Catholic masses for the Cuban people.

1999 Elián Gonzalez is rescued and taken to the United States after his mother drowns fleeing Cuba in November.

Castro demands the return of Elián Gonzalez to Cuba.

2002 Castro hosts a visit by former U.S. President Jimmy Carter.

2003 Castro has almost eighty people he considers to be political opponents arrested and imprisoned.

To Find Out More

BOOKS

Bourne, Peter. *Fidel: A Biography of Fidel Castro.* New York: Dodd, Mead & Company, 1986.

Castro Ruz, Fidel. *Fidel: My Early Years.* Melbourne: Ocean Press, 1998.

Matthews, Herbert L. *Fidel Castro.* New York: Simon & Schuster, 1969.

Meneses, Enrique. *Fidel Castro.* New York: Taplinger Publishing Co., Inc., 1968.

Quirk, Robert. *Fidel Castro.* New York: W. W. Norton Co., 1993.

Selsdon, Esther. *The Life and Times of Fidel Castro.* Broomall, PA: Chelsea House Publishers, 1997.

Szulc, Tad. *Fidel: A Critical Portrait.* New York: William Morrow and Co., Inc., 1986.

ORGANIZATIONS AND ONLINE SITES

Castro Speech Databases
http://www.lanic.utexas.edu/la/cb/cuba/castro.html

This site contains a search engine that allows the user to search through Castro's speeches, from the 1950s to the 1990s.

Digital Granma Internacional
http://www.granma.cu/ingles/index.html

This is the official site for the *Granma*, the newspaper representing Cuba, and Castro's, perspective on national and international events. It offers an interesting perspective from the other point of view.

Free Cuba Foundation
http://www.fiu.edu/~fcf/

This is the site of an anti-Castro organization that lists Castro's human rights abuses and failure to bring democracy to Cuba.

The Fortieth Anniversary of the Cuban Revolution
http://www.seeingred.com/2.3/fidel.html

This site contains the full text of a speech Castro gave on the fortieth anniversary of the Cuban Revolution. He sets out his most recent critique of capitalism in the modern world.

A Note on Sources

Castro has been the subject of countless books, papers, and articles, including yesterday's headlines, since he ascended the world stage more than forty years ago. He also excites enormous controversy, and finding balanced judgments of his character and record are difficult. Three journalists interviewed Castro and watched him at work during the early part of his rule: Herbert Matthews for *The New York Times*, Enrique Meneses for Paris *Match*, and Lee Lockwood, a photojournalist. All three published fascinating descriptions of the rebel leader, though all three were also criticized for portraying him positively and not addressing Castro's abuse of power. Castro gave his own version of his childhood, *Fidel: My Early Years*, which is inaccurate in many points, but shows the spirit of a leader who never gave up. To get a more complete picture of Castro, I read Robert Quirk's *Fidel Castro* and Tad Szulc's *Fidel Castro: A Critical Portrait*. I used Quirk's brilliant account as the source for many of the anecdotes in the book. Both books give detailed descriptions of Castro's human rights abuses and repressive rule. Since Castro still holds a distinctive position in world affairs today, the reader can keep up with his ideas and actions in newspapers or on the *Granma* website, the Cuban national paper that reflects Castro's views. For the Elián controversy, I relied upon newspaper accounts in the *Miami Herald* and *The New York Times*. Overviews and quotes used from participants were drawn from the excellent documentary "Saving Elián" by PBS's *Frontline*.

—*Brendan January*

Index

About the Author

Brendan January is an award-winning author of more than twenty-five nonfiction books for young readers. January was educated at Haverford College, where he earned a B.A. in history and English, and at the Columbia Graduate School of Journalism. He is a Fulbright Scholar and lives with his wife and daughter in New York City and Berlin.